I0157608

"We lived, felt dawn, saw sunset glow...."

Copyright ©2011, 2014 Dolores H. Lees & James T. Lees

All rights reserved. Without limiting the rights under copyright reserved above,
no part of this publication may be reproduced, stored in or introduced into a retrieval system,
or transmitted in any form or by any means (electronic, mechanical, photocopying,
recording or otherwise), without the prior written permission of the copyright owners.
Cover and interior design by Mountain View Media © 2011, 2014

Cataloging in Publication Data: 394.264
Lees, Dolores H., 1949 –
Lees, James T., 1947 –

Second Edition
Printed and bound in The United States of America

ISBN: 978-0-9739848-2-8

1. Remembrance Day (Canada) –Juvenile Literature
2. Canada – History, Military – Juvenile Literature
3. History - World War Two - Canada

JAEDA
COMMUNICATIONS

46262 Greenwood Drive
Chilliwack, British Columbia, Canada

My Two Great Grandfathers
A Story of Remembrance

Dolores H. Lees
James T. Lees

For Davis,
And his two great grandfathers,
James David Henry Templeton
and Thomas George Lees

Contents

Royal Canadian Legion Cemetery, Chilliwack, British Columbia

THEIR NAME LIVETH FOR EVERMORE

My Story of Remembrance

My name is Davis and I live in a peaceful country called Canada.

I just learned about Remembrance Day. I found out about it because my two great grandfathers fought in World War II.

Your grandparents or great grandparents may be part of the Remembrance Day story too.

My grandmother told me about it first...

My Two Great Grandfathers

Great Grandpa Jim
James David Henry Templeton
Born 1923 – Died 2013
Birthplace: Lajord, Saskatchewan

Great Grandpa Tommy
Thomas George Lees
Born 1920 – Died 1981
Birthplace: Oyen, Alberta

These are my two great grandfathers who fought in World War II. Great Grandpa Tommy joined the Canadian Army in 1940 and Great Grandpa Jim joined the Royal Canadian Air Force in 1943. They fought in the war so that we could live in a free country.

They are part of my story about Remembrance Day.

Great Grandpa Jim's Story

I grew up on a big farm in Saskatchewan. When I was young, I wanted to be a farmer, but the war was on, and being the eldest son in the family, I decided to join the war effort.

In February 1943 I joined the Royal Canadian Air Force. I went to Moose Jaw for basic engine mechanic training. I was sent to St. Thomas, Ontario to a technical training school and from there I was posted to the No. 4 Service Flying Training School in Saskatoon. While there, I worked as a mechanic servicing airplanes. It was just a few kilometers from home, so I used to go home every other weekend for a visit.

Later, I went to Brandon for boot camp. They taught us how to walk and how to march, but it had nothing to do with working on airplane engines.

Here I am with my mom and my dad on one of my visits home before going to Europe.

In March 1944, I was sent to Winnipeg. They put us into a Sunday parade. There were 101 of us from the air force, navy, army, and even some paratroopers. Everybody marched, nine abreast, in front of some dignitaries and the Governor General.

Parade Day in Winnipeg

After being in Winnipeg for about six months, I volunteered to go overseas. It was September 1944. We had to travel by ship and I went over on the *Isle de France,* a ship carrying 12 000 troops. That was a terrible trip across the North Atlantic. The waves were higher than the boat, and we were put up in hammocks five high, two decks below the water line. We were freezing all the time. The first two days out we had a fighter escort, the middle two days we were on our own, and the last two days we had a fighter escort from England. During the whole trip we changed course every six minutes to avoid submarine torpedoes. Many of us were very sea sick.

After six days we finally got to Scotland. We landed just outside of Glasgow. We rode in the back of trucks to England, where I got posted outside of York to Number 6 Bomber Command. I worked on four-engine Halifax bombers but soon we switched to Canadian Lancasters with Merlin engines. As an air engine mechanic, I went up flying with the pilot to check the engine in flight. While on those flights we climbed to 10 000 meters, then dropped down to 15 meters. The bombadier would drop a smoke bomb, and the air gunners had gunnery practice. This took place over the North Sea.

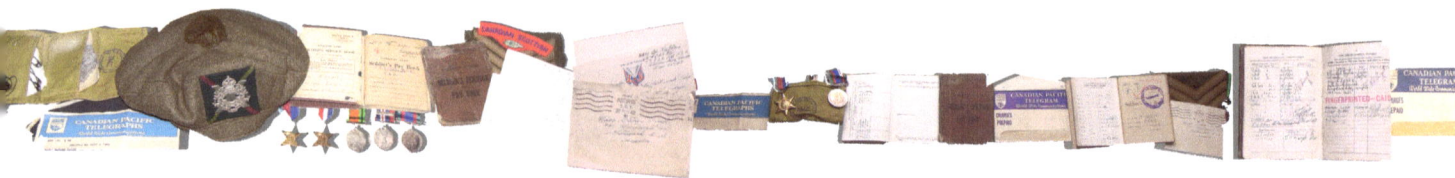

We were able to send telegrams home saying that we were okay. I started writing letters home nearly every day. I numbered them, so that we would know if some went missing. Once, some of my letters sent home were partially burned in a plane crash, but they were still delivered because the addresses could be read. There wasn't much left of the letters though.

They issued us a battle jacket, but we kept the same uniform. They never gave us any overalls, so if we ever got into any grease, or other chemicals, they had to be cleaned with gasoline or aviation gas. It wasn't too bad in bomber command, we didn't get into very much grease. When we got posted to the transport squadron, we had a lot more work to do, and our uniforms did get dirty. We had a barrel of gas outside the shop, and we would dunk our clothes in there, wash them out, and hang them up on a line to dry to get all the smell out. Then we would wear them again. At this time, we were living in Quonset huts. They were all metal, and were divided into two. Each half had an old stove that burned coke - a very poor grade of coal. It didn't burn well, so we used to take some of the high-powered aviation gasoline to mix with the coke, and we always had nice fires. We never burned the place down either.

10

I was assigned to a single plane as an airframe mechanic and instrument mechanic. I would have to fill them with gas for a mission. Sometimes they would change their minds, and I'd have to drain so many liters of gas out because they weren't going to fly as far. Then they'd change their minds again, so I'd have to fill them up again. I even bought a bike to ride out to the plane to fill it up because it was so far to walk!

Once they took off, we'd have to stay in this hut until they came back. When the flight crew returned and were all settled in, we could go have something to eat and go to bed. Then we would get up and get ready for the next mission.

When on leave, I visited my Dad's relatives at Kilwinning, Scotland (four aunts, Annie, Tina, Mary, Margaret and two uncles, Sandy and David).

Other times I would visit my cousins Cathy and Arnold, just outside of London. She had a daughter, and I used to take her some chocolate bars, which people were good enough to send to me from home. One time when I was in London I walked around seeing all the sights, like Picadilly Circus, and the Tube system (the subway) which was really great.

Avro Lancaster bomber: Many were built in Canada, using the Merlin engines

I was on leave in London one time, just walking around, and somebody said the war was over. It was May 8,1945, V-E Day. Victory in Europe. After years of blackouts – so enemy bombers couldn't see the city – everybody was waiting for the lights to come back on, but they didn't until quite a few days later. On V-E day I walked into the southeast part of London, the part that was really bombed. There was nothing but holes there.

Just after Victory in Europe Day (VE Day), I took this photograph at Buckingham Palace.

One day soon after, I walked to Buckingham Palace, and the King (George VI), the Queen and the two Princesses came out and waved, and everyone waved back. One of the princesses is now Queen Elizabeth. That was a holiday.

Since the war in Europe was over, I was posted to Down Ampney, England to a transport squadron and worked on old DC3 Dakota two-engine transport planes. They were flying food and supplies over to Europe to replace what they lost due to all the bombing.

This is a DC-3, also known as a C-47, which we called a "Dakota" transport plane. Some of these planes are still flying.

The *Ile de France,* which I traveled on to and from Great Britain

It was April of 1946 before I got home. I came home on the *Isle de France*. It was a calm six day trip. I was discharged in June of 1946; I could have stayed in the Air Force but I'd had enough of it...then I found there were no jobs. The better jobs were taken by people who had stayed in Canada.

I worked on my folks' farm until November 20, 1946. That was the day I married my wartime sweetheart. Eventually, I found work moving animal hides to tanneries, where they made leather. It wasn't a very good job. I also had many other jobs.

In 1980 I returned to visit England, Scotland and Wales. I also managed to include a one day trip to Dieppe, France.

I am happy that I served in World War II, and that I was able to help my country. I feel honored to live in a peaceful and free country.

Great-Grandpa Tommy's Story

I was only 19 years old when World War II started. We were living in B.C. One of my older brothers, Andy, an engineer, joined the army. I always admired my brother, so I decided to join the army too. I signed up with the Canadian Army on September 30, 1940. I really believed I was joining "to fight for the right that we might be able to live as one in peace and comfort." That's what we were told, over and over.

I was sent to Vancouver, to a temporary camp in Stanley Park. There were 120 officers and men in that camp. We had three huts, a mess hall - that's where we ate - and a shower we could use every second day. It wasn't so bad. It was like camping.

This convoy is just about to leave Nova Scotia on its voyage to Britain.
It will be guarded by the allied navies, and by the air forces when it is near enough to land.

In May, 1941, I left by train and travelled to Halifax, then was put on a troop ship in a convoy to Great Britain. It took six days.

I was in England from May 1941 to June 1944. For a long time, we had no leaves, or "time off," and spent time keeping our guns clean and oiled. If we didn't, the guns would rust because of the English rain. We wrote letters home, but couldn't send many photographs. We couldn't write just anything we wanted in our letters home either. There were special rules for everything, and all our letters were read, and checked before they could be sent.

By November, I was promoted to Lance Bombardier, with a pay raise. I got one stripe on my shoulder with the new rank.

Here I am with my anti-aircraft gun in southern England

Christmas dinner in 1941 wasn't much like the ones at home. We got roast pork, some chicken and a little turkey. Winter was cold and dark, but by February, 1942 we got a radio and electric lights. No more oil lamps for us! We got a camp library, and I was put in charge.

Our conditions got even better in May. We moved to a new site near the town of Gillingham in the southern part of England, and we could leave our tents behind. Now we had huts, running hot and cold water, showers, and linoleum on the floors. Gillingham was near Rochester, where we could go roller skating when we had leave. Here we were in the middle of a war, and we could go roller skating!

Usually there were training and fitness drills, but on Sundays we had the day off. We could get up late, clean our rooms, then play softball, go for a walk or watch cricket. This was our summer of 1942.

In the fall, some of the boys helped out with the harvesting of crops. Many of us were farm boys from Canada anyway, so we knew how to work. We were out of shape though. Harvesting was done by hand a lot of the time. I was stacking oats with a pitchfork and got blisters.

I got engaged to your great grandmother that fall too. She was in Canada. I proposed in a letter, then my mother bought the ring for me and delivered it. It wasn't very romantic.

1943 didn't start well for me. We were sleeping outside, and I nearly froze. I got frostbite on my ears. The army was printing a daily newspaper called "Advance Post." They could print newspapers, but I was sleeping on the ground and freezing. Maybe they were preparing us for the next stage of the war.

Helping with the harvest

Soon I was promoted to Acting Sergeant, with higher pay. Now I was making $2.20 per day. I could save quite a lot of money. In May 1943, I became a Lance Sergeant in the artillery.

The same month, I met my brothers, Andy and Jimmy in London, England. I hadn't seen Jimmy for years. We had a good time, and didn't worry too much about the bombs which continued to fall near us. We didn't talk about bombing cities at all, because Jimmy was a bomber pilot in the Royal Canadian Air Force.

I remember going to a show in Brighton, also in the south of England, in the early fall. It was in the theater we heard that Italy had surrendered, although the fighting would go on with the Germans still occupying that country. Still, it was good news to us.

In October we were sent on a training course in Wales. We travelled in the back of a truck, but since I helped the driver, I got more comfortable seating in the cab. I also helped spell off a motorcycle driver. I enjoyed that. I didn't enjoy Wales that much though. We slept under canvas, in the bush, in the almost steady rain. We were always soaking wet and cold. Dinner was sandwiches.

Our gun crew in Southern England

Just before Christmas, both Jimmy and I got leave. After meeting him in Edinburgh, Scotland, we both went to Morebattle, where we had relatives. It was the best Christmas in Britain so far.

In 1944 I was back on base. We now had fresh fruit; mainly oranges. What a treat. The weather was better, and even though it was January, two of us borrowed motorcycles and took a long ride into the English countryside.

Along with better food, we also got new guns. That could only mean a new mission was planned. That would be D-Day. We were stationed in Bournemouth, waiting. I remember that the only thing I looked forward to, and got enjoyment out of, was reading letters from home, over and over. We got parcels too, with tea bags, nuts, gum, canned meat, chocolate bars and homemade candy. We even got soap, socks and sweaters.

By 1944 we knew the invasion of German-controlled Europe was near, and it would be very dangerous.

June 6, 1944: I landed with thousands of Canadian soldiers on Juno Beach in Normandy, France. The invasion began.

A couple of weeks later, we were moving through France, living in tents, cooking outside, using washbasins instead of showers and sleeping in shifts. Today, some people do this for fun, and call it hiking or camping. This wasn't fun; it was still a war. We did get some rest. In September, I got to visit with Jimmy in Scotland.

Christmas dinner in France, 1944 – I was surprised. It was a feast! We had cold turkey and pork, gravy, applesauce, peas, brussels sprouts, mashed potatoes and plum pudding with sauce.

We were living in a house in France by the middle of January 1945. There was no electricity; we were back to using oil lamps. It was my job to operate our phone system. Letters from home were only taking seven to ten days to arrive by this time.

On May 8, 1945, the war in Europe was officially over, but it took us three more weeks to work our way to Amsterdam, in the Netherlands. Even though the war in the Pacific would continue until August, we would finally be going home.

My brother Jimmy was killed transporting fighter planes back to North Dakota at the end of the war. Andy became an oil company executive in Calgary.

I eventually moved to Chilliwack, British Columbia. I always attend a Remembrance Day ceremony. It reminds me that every single day we should remember why we live in peace and why we should be grateful.

I didn't ever go back to Europe.

Jimmy, Andy and Tommy, all in uniform

19

Lest We Forget

We need to remember, recognize and thank all the veterans who served during WWII and all other wars in order that we can live in our peaceful country today.

Canadian War Memorial
Ottawa, Ontario

Left: memorial statue
in Lenore, Manitoba

Remembrance Day

I was sad when I found out that Remembrance Day started because of the Great War. When this war ended, a peace document was signed. This document was called an armistice and all fighting would stop at 11:00 a.m. on November 11, 1918.

The first Remembrance Day was held on November 11, 1919. This day was called Armistice Day. Everyone stopped their work and activities for 2 minutes of silence.

Now on Remembrance Day we honor the Canadians who stood up for freedom and peace in the world in wars, United Nations missions and peacekeeping missions.

FACT:
Armistice Day was officially renamed Remembrance Day in 1931.

Remembrance Day Parade, Chilliwack, British Columbia

In Flanders Fields

In Flanders fields the poppies blow
Between the crosses, row on row,
That mark our place; and in the sky
The larks, still bravely singing, fly
Scarce heard amid the guns below.

We are the Dead. Short days ago
We lived, felt dawn, saw sunset glow,
Loved, and were loved, and now we lie
In Flanders fields.

Take up our quarrel with the foe:
To you from failing hands we throw
The torch; be yours to hold it high.
If ye break faith with us who die
We shall not sleep, though poppies grow
In Flanders fields.

by John McCrae, 1915

Lt. Colonel John McCrae

In Flanders Fields

—

In Flanders fields the poppies grow
Between the crosses, row on row
That mark our place : and in the sky
The larks still ...
Scarce heard a...

We are the Dead...
We lived, felt...
Loved, and were...
In Flanders fie...

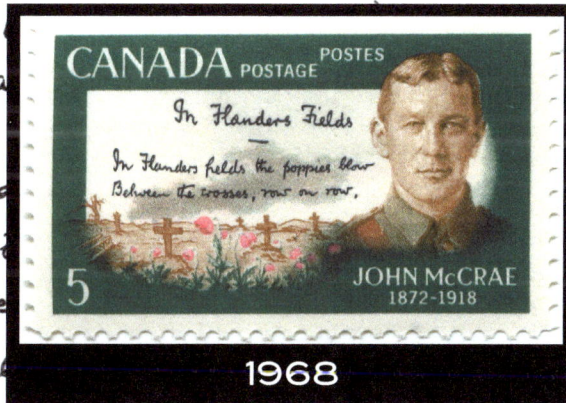

CANADA POSTAGE POSTES

In Flanders Fields

In Flanders fields the poppies blow
Between the crosses, row on row,

5

JOHN McCRAE
1872-1918

1968

Take up our quarrel with the foe :
To you from failing hands we throw
The Torch : be yours to hold it high !
If ye break faith with us who die
We shall not sleep, though poppies grow
In Flanders fields.

John McCrae

Above: John McCrae, at home in Ontario, about 1912

Because of the poem by Lt. Col. John McCrae, the poppy became famous. McCrae was a doctor from Ontario. He died from pneumonia and menningitis in January, 1918.

23

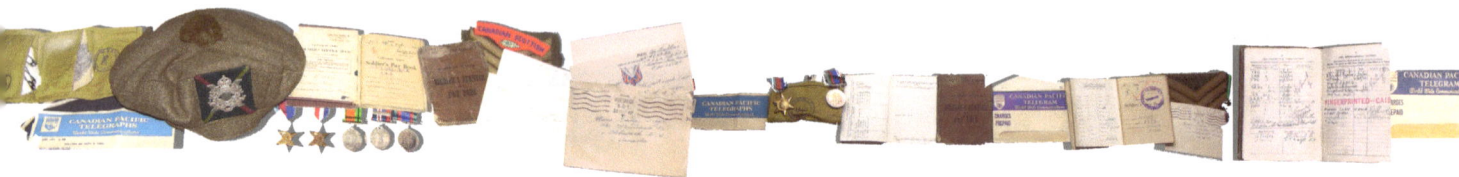

The Poppy

I'm told that we don't remember wars, but we remember the men and women who were involved in the wars. They risked their lives so that we could be free.

There are many symbols of Remembrance Day and I learned that the red poppy is the most famous of them. They grow wild in parts of France and Belgium, especially in the cemeteries over thousands of graves. Poppies are especially common in the northern Belgian provinces called Flanders. Poppies became a symbol because of the famous poem written by Colonel John McCrae.

It must be strange to see all those bright, cheerful, colorful flowers growing in such a sad place.

Wild poppies growing in Scotland

A Symbol of Remembrance Day

In November 1921 Canada chose to use the poppy as a symbol of remembrance and as a way to raise money for veterans in need.

Poppies are sold by the Royal Canadian Legion to help veterans. Some veterans need help with medical services, or even for housing and food. Injured veterans often depended on this. Each year, the Legion raises over $1 million.

The poppy is worn on the left lapel or as close to the heart as possible. It can also be worn on a cap or hat. We wear poppies to remember all of the Canadians who have lost their lives trying to help others. We must never forget that we live in peace because brave people went to war and risked their lives to protect us.

Symbols of Remembrance: Stamps

Canada 50 — Battle of the Atlantic · Bataille de l'Atlantique

Canadian War Museum · Musée Canadien de la Guerre — lest we forget — CANADA 50 — n'oublions jamais

2005

1918-1968 — 15 — POSTES CANADA POSTAGE

1968

Canada 49 — 06.06.44 — D-Day · Jour J — Juno Beach, Normandy · Plage Juno, Normandie

2004

Avro Lancaster — Postes Postage — Canada 17

198C

CANADA — POSTES POSTAGE — 1939 — CENTS — 1

1939

AIR FORCE/LES FORCES AÉRIENNES — CANADA 32

1984

Symbols of Remembrance:
Coins & Money

Can you find these Canadian coins?

5¢	2005	"V" for victory re-issue
25¢	2004	With a red poppy
25¢	2010	With two red poppies - Remembrance Day
$1	1994	National War Memorial
$1	1995	Peacekeepers
$1	2010	Navy & Merchant Marine

Poem inset on the Canadian Ten Dollar Bill

In Flanders fields the poppies blow
Between the crosses, row on row,
That mark our place; and in the sky
The larks, still bravely singing, fly
Scarce heard amid the guns below.
John McCrae 1872-1918

Au champ d'honneur les coquelicots
Sont parsemés de lot en lot,
Auprès des croix; et dans l'espace
Les alouettes devenues lasses
Mêlent leurs chants au sifflement
Des obusiers.

More Symbols of Remembrance

Canadian National Vimy Memorial, Pas de Calais, France

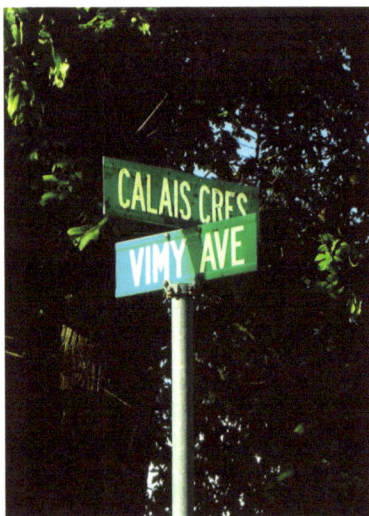

Book of Remembrance, Ottawa

Street signs
Canada Education Park,
Chilliwack, BC

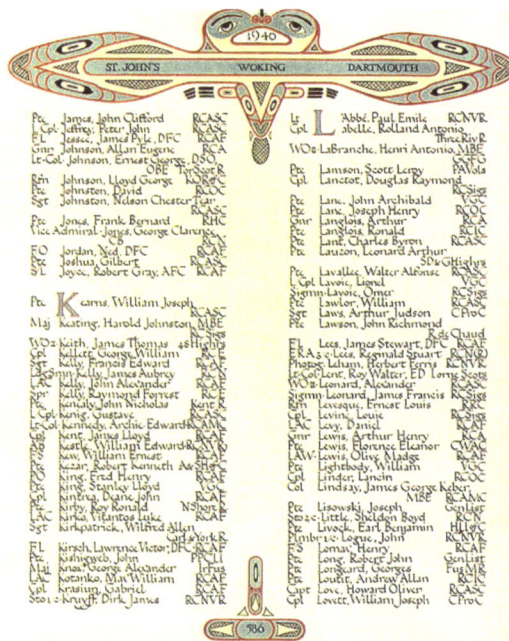

Vehicle Licence Plate, BC

The Canadian Navy and Merchant Marine

The Battle of the Atlantic
September 3, 1939 – May 7, 1945

The Battle of the Atlantic lasted the whole European war, involving 14 nations. Most of the fighting started with German submarines attacking Allied ships, and with Allied warships and aircraft destroying the submarines. Defeating the submarines was necessary to keep food and supplies going to Britain, and to prepare for the D-Day invasion.

At first, most of the Allied ships were protected by British and Canadian warships and air forces. Later, the United States joined the convoys and provided protection too. About 1/3 of the German submarines were destroyed by Lancaster bombers while they were still in port.

There were over 100 convoy battles, and about 1000 individual submarine attacks. Newly invented sonar helped locate submarines, but it wasn't very accurate at first.

Allied Losses in the Battle of the Atlantic:
30 264 merchant sailors
3500 merchant vessels
175 warships
119 aircraft
28 000 sailors

The German Navy lost 783 submarines and many of their other warships.

Canadian Corvette K131, known as HMCS Chilliwack – used to hunt and destroy U-boats (submarines)

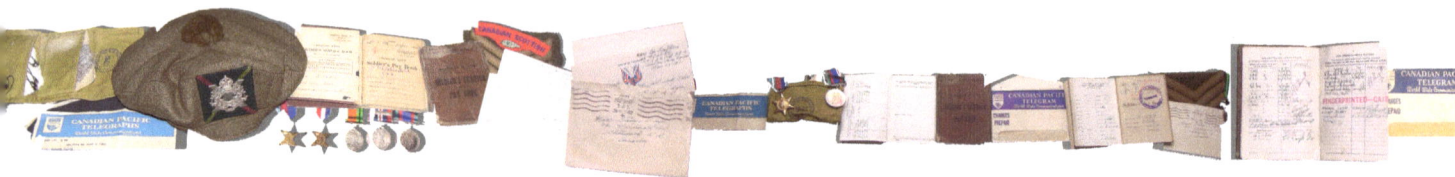

Scrapbook

Canadian service medals

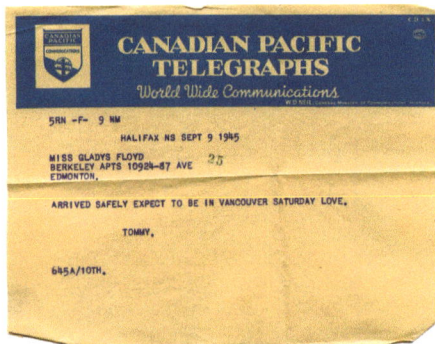

Telegraph: coming home at last

CANADIAN SCOTTISH

Shoulder patch

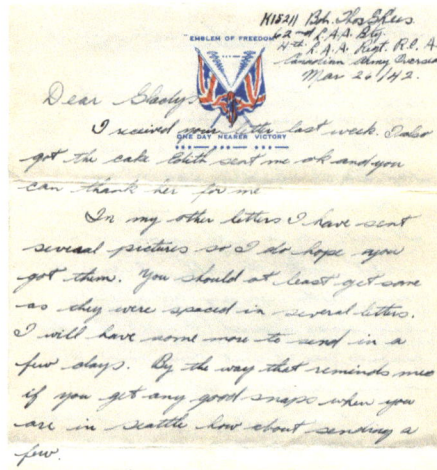

A letter from the front

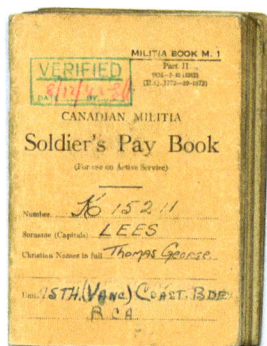

Record of payment for soldiers

Cap (beret) badge:
Canadian Scottish Regiment

Supermarine Spitfire fighter plane from the Battle of Britain

I Won't Forget

I won't forget that my two brave
great grandfathers fought
in the Second World War,
and I will always appreciate
the freedoms we have today.

Thank you Great Grandpa Jim and
Great Grandpa Tommy.

Thank you to all the veterans still alive today.

We must remember.

Sources & Acknowledgements

Photographs © 2011 by Dolores H. Lees & James T. Lees: *Inside cover, contents page, and pages 6, 20 (memorial statue) 21,24, 25, 27 (coins) and 28 (street signs).*

Photographs property of James David Henry Templeton, used by permission: *pages 7, 8, 9, 10, and 13, Front cover, photographer(s) unknown. Page 12, Buckingham Palace, by James D. H. Templeton.*

Photographs property of the Thomas George Lees estate, used by permission: *pages 7, 14, 16, 17, 18, 19 (all three) and 30 (Spitfire), Front cover, photographer(s) unknown. Images on page 30 © James T. Lees and Dolores H. Lees.*

Back cover photograph by Antonio Quesada M, used by permission (www.publicdomainpictures.net)

Front cover poppy photograph by Patricia Crosstown, used by permission (www.publicdomainpictures.net)

Page 11, Lancaster bomber, Bigstock.com, used by permission under license

Page 12, DC3 / Dakota, photo by Max Haynes - MaxAir2Air.com, used by permission

Page 13, Ile de France, Original photographer source unknown

Page 15, Atlantic Convoy, Canada, Department of National Defence / Library and Archives Canada, used by permission

Page 20, National War Memorial, Mediafocus, used by permission under license

Page 22, In Flanders Fields, is in public domain

Page 23, Lt. Colonel John McCrae, is in public domain

Pages 23 and 26, images of Canadian Postage Stamps © Canada Post

Page 27, images of the Canadian $10 banknote courtesy of the Bank of Canada, used by permission

Page 28, Vimy Ridge Memorial, reproduced with the permission of Veterans Affairs Canada, 2011

Page 28, Book of Remembrance, public domain

Page 29, Corvette K131 photographer and source unknown

We welcome information relating to images for which the source or creator is unknown so that credit may be given wherever possible.

NM
MOUNTAIN VIEW MEDIA

www.ingramcontent.com/pod-product-compliance
Lightning Source LLC
Chambersburg PA
CBHW042106040426
42448CB00002B/156

9780973984828